THE LIFE OF JESUS—I AM

Retreat Leader Guide
WORKBOOK

RICHARD T. CASE

To my wife, Linda, who has faithfully walked with me and our family in

understanding and receiving the Life of Jesus as the Great "I AM".

She has always been a faithful learner and receiver of the Names of God.

She particularly had us spend time learning and receiving the depth of

Christ's statements about Himself as the Great I AM"—

"I AM" THE BREAD OF LIFE,

"I AM" THE LIGHT OF THE WORLD,

"I AM" THE DOOR/GATE to ABUNDANT LIFE,

"I AM" THE GOOD SHEPHERD,

"I AM" THE RESURRECTION AND THE LIFE,

"I AM" THE WAY, THE TRUTH, AND THE LIFE,

"I AM" THE TRUE VINE.

Together, we studied and processed each statement and then

applied the truths of who Christ is to our lives—as He then live this life

out through us. It has been a joy to experience this and walk together

into the profound truths of the Life of Christ. She is truly a woman of

encouragement that seeks to enjoy the great "I AM".

Acknowledgments

We wish to thank all of the leaders of our **Ministry: Living Waters—ABIDE Ministries!** These leaders have also learned what it means to understand and receive the Life of the Great I AM: They have been shining examples of bearing witness to this life and giving this away to others—who then are learning to also explore and receive the Great "I AM".

These leaders are:

Jake & Mary Beckel
Rich & Janet Cocchiaro
Larry & Sherry Collet
Scott & Kristen Cornell
David & Melissa Dunkel
Tom & Susanne Ewing
Rick & Kelly Ferris
Joel & Christina Gunn
Rick & Nancy Hoover
Don & Rachelle Light
Chris and Heidi May
Steve & Carolyn Van Ooteghem
Preston & Lynda Pitts
Dan & Kathy Rocconi
Bob & Keri Rockwell
Allyson & Denny Weinberg

THE LIFE OF JESUS—I AM
ABIDE MINISTRIES
7615 Lemon Gulch Way
Castle Rock, CO 80108

ISBN: 979-8-218-32047-8

Publisher's Cataloging-in-Publication data

Names:
Title:
Description: .
Identifiers: ISBN | LCCN
Subjects:

Printed in the United States of America 2023 — 1st ed

TABLE OF CONTENTS

INTRODUCTION

Welcome to our course, *The Life of Jesus—I Am*. This study was developed primarily out of the Gospel of John. John wrote about Jesus, understanding that Jesus spoke of Himself as "I am." In this study we will learn that certain truths describe His nature—and in essence that the "I am" means I am everything. We're going to look at this life and what it means to us—receiving and living this life. It's a very exciting study of understanding the nature and character of Christ's life and the opportunity for us to enjoy that life.

Read John 20:30–31:

The Purpose of This Book
[30] Now Jesus did many other signs in the presence of the disciples, which are not written in this book; [31] but these are written so that you may believe that Jesus is the Christ, the Son of God, and that by believing you may have life in his name.

____

____

____

____

____

John said: Everything that has been written here is for what purpose? That we might believe that Jesus is who He says He is. Not only are we to believe it but also to experience it. It's not to learn about Jesus. It's to understand the nature of Jesus and the knowing of Jesus—it is experiencing Jesus. Why do we have the privilege of experiencing Him? Because He lives inside us. By definition, as believers, our purpose is to experience His life because He's already there.

Read John 8:54–59:

[54] Jesus answered, "If I glorify myself, my glory is nothing. It is my Father who glorifies me, of whom you say, 'He is our God.'[a] [55] But you have not known him. I know him. If I were to say that I do not know him, I would be a liar like you, but I do know him and I keep his word. [56] Your father Abraham rejoiced that he would see my day. He saw it and was glad." [57] So the Jews said to him, "You are not yet fifty years old, and have you seen Abraham?"[b] [58] Jesus said to them, "Truly, truly, I say to you, before Abraham was, I am." [59] So they picked up stones to throw at him, but Jesus hid himself and went out of the temple.

The Jews who were listening to Jesus speak asked Him a question: Who are you? Jesus made a statement when He responded, "Before Abraham was, I am." He switched tenses. He didn't say: Before Abraham was, I was too. He says, "Before Abraham was, I am." He is God eternal. What does the "I am" mean? It's all of God—all His names—eternal. This is a great example of how abiding draws us deeper into truth. When you read that Jesus said "I am," what would be your natural question? You are what? "I am who I am." What does "I am" mean? This study will explore exactly what "I am" means. We will look at the "I am" in various dimensions, and we will learn to understand the depth of this—not just intellectually but experientially.

Read Exodus 3:12–18:

12 He said, "But I will be with you, and this shall be the sign for you, that I have sent you: when you have brought the people out of Egypt, you shall serve God on this mountain."

13 Then Moses said to God, "If I come to the people of Israel and say to them, 'The God of your fathers has sent me to you,' and they ask me, 'What is his name?' what shall I say to them?" 14 God said to Moses, "I AM WHO I AM."[a] And he said, "Say this to the people of Israel: 'I AM has sent me to you.'" 15 God also said to Moses, "Say this to the people of Israel: 'The LORD,[b] the God of your fathers, the God of Abraham, the God of Isaac, and the God of Jacob, has sent me to you.' This is my name forever, and thus I am to be remembered throughout all generations. 16 Go and gather the elders of Israel together and say to them, 'The LORD, the God of your fathers, the God of Abraham, of Isaac, and of Jacob, has appeared to me, saying, "I have observed you and what has been done to you in Egypt, 17 and I promise that I will bring you up out of the affliction of Egypt to the land of the Canaanites, the Hittites, the Amorites, the Perizzites, the Hivites, and the Jebusites, a land flowing with milk and honey."' 18 And they will listen to your voice, and you and the elders of Israel shall go to the king of Egypt and say to him, 'The LORD, the God of the Hebrews, has met with us; and now, please let us go a three days' journey into the wilderness, that we may sacrifice to the LORD our God.'

God told Moses that He was sending him to Pharoah to orchestrate freeing the nation of Israel from slavery. Moses said, "Who am I that I should go to Pharoah and bring the Israelites out of Egypt?" God confirmed that Moses was who He had chosen to carry this out and also told Moses that this was about Him, not Moses.

Moses then asks God who he should say sends him? He knows he's talking to God. His understanding of God is Elohim—God is all powerful. He's essentially telling God, "I know who You are, but who exactly should I say You are to the Israelites and to Pharaoh?" God's answers: Tell them, "I am the I am." God says His name is "I am." It is personal, and it is all powerful. So, Moses was to tell them that "I am" sent him. Though this is a new understanding, God will reveal and demonstrate the truth and fullness of "I am."

Read Matthew 14:22–33:

Jesus Walks on the Water

[22] Immediately he made the disciples get into the boat and go before him to the other side, while he dismissed the crowds. [23] And after he had dismissed the crowds, he went up on the mountain by himself to pray. When evening came, he was there alone, [24] but the boat by this time was a long way[a] from the land,[b] beaten by the waves, for the wind was against them. [25] And in the fourth watch of the night[c] he came to them, walking on the sea. [26] But when the disciples saw him walking on the sea, they were terrified, and said, "It is a ghost!" and they cried out in fear. [27] But immediately Jesus spoke to them, saying, "Take heart; it is I. Do not be afraid."

[28] And Peter answered him, "Lord, if it is you, command me to come to you on the water." [29] He said, "Come." So Peter got out of the boat and walked on the water and came to Jesus. [30] But when he saw the wind,[d] he was afraid, and beginning to sink he cried out, "Lord, save me." [31] Jesus immediately reached out his hand and took hold of him, saying to him, "O you of little faith, why did you doubt?" [32] And when they got into the boat, the wind ceased. [33] And those in the boat worshiped him, saying, "Truly you are the Son of God."

Unfortunately, this is an example of where the English language doesn't quite capture the truth of the Greek. Jesus sends His disciples out according to His will. (We have two courses: *Discerning God's Will* and *Discerning God's Will Part 2* that are worthwhile to understand the truths and process of living out God's will for us personally.) Where did He send them? Into a storm. For what reason? He is about to show them something. What is He about to show them? He is going to show them about the nature and character of Jesus.

When you are praying, be careful not to ask God to spare you from storms and troubles. Rather, ask God to have you experience Him wherever He sends you. When you are going through trials, you will have the privilege of seeing something new about God and experiencing Him.

The disciples are in the boat, and they are in trouble. In addition, they're greatly afraid. And when they see this being walking on the water, this scares them even more. In the English translation, Jesus calls out and says, "Do not be afraid, it is I." However, in the Greek, it says, "Do not be afraid, I am." With this, the disciples understood that Jesus said, "I am here, and I will take care of this—I am." Peter says, "If you're really 'I am,' then have me come out to you." Jesus confirmed and told Peter to come on out.

Given the circumstances, it took a great deal of faith for Peter to get out of the boat. When he gets out, he starts walking—supernaturally. Jesus didn't put rocks in the right place, and Jesus wasn't next to him—it was truly supernatural that Peter was able to walk on water at that moment. As soon as Peter turned his attention to the storm and the difficult—impossible—circumstances, he stopped focusing on Jesus and started to sink. He called out to Jesus to save him, and Jesus reached down, took him by the hand, and pulled him up. Jesus knew that Peter had gone as far as he could given the limit of his faith, so He took care of him. Jesus then walked him back to the boat—again supernaturally on the water. Peter walked on the water because he was with Jesus—he was with the "I am."

> **Read Hebrews 11:6:**
>
> [6] And without faith it is impossible to please him, for whoever would draw near to God must believe that he exists and that he rewards those who seek him.

____

____

____

____

Without faith, it's impossible to please God. We are called to walk a life of faith—all the time. Difficulties, struggles, storms, etc. are not to bother us because by faith, we know that God will provide resolution. This verse goes on to say what? It says that he who comes to God must believe that He exists and that He is a reward for those who diligently seek Him. Unfortunately, this is another example where the English translation does not capture the full meaning. It's impossible to live without faith because life is always going to require faith. It would be much easier for God to put you in a spot where you are completely safe, but God says that your life's going to be dangerous, it's going to be full of tribulation, and you're always going to have to require faith to believe what He has to say. He says the key is that you believe that He is—that He exists.

The Hebrew doesn't say that. It says you must believe that God is—that He exists—and that He is the "I am." If you believe that He is the "I am," then He will reward those who diligently seek Him. Who will provide the reward? The "I am." What's the reward? To give you what is needed to please God—faith. If you believe that He is "I am," and diligently seek Him to experience Him as "I am," then He will give you faith. Without faith, it is what? Impossible to please Him. So, to please Him, we need faith, and if we believe He is "I am," He will give us what we need. The reward is faith. He will give us the faith to believe what He has to say.

"Jesus supernaturally fed the 5,000 through multiplying it in the baskets He's just demonstrated that the spiritual supersedes the physical—and that He can do remarkable things."

The Bread of Life:

Jesus referred to Himself as the Bread of Life. What does that mean? What then are we to do with this bread? How do we fulfill this? Why is this so crucial to how we live out His life in us?

Read John 6:22–40; 47–51:

I Am the Bread of Life

22 On the next day the crowd that remained on the other side of the sea saw that there had been only one boat there, and that Jesus had not entered the boat with his disciples, but that his disciples had gone away alone. 23 Other boats from Tiberias came near the place where they had eaten the bread after the Lord had given thanks. 24 So when the crowd saw that Jesus was not there, nor his disciples, they themselves got into the boats and went to Capernaum, seeking Jesus.

25 When they found him on the other side of the sea, they said to him, "Rabbi, when did you come here?" 26 Jesus answered them, "Truly, truly, I say to you, you are seeking me, not because you saw signs, but because you ate your fill of the loaves. 27 Do not work for the food that perishes, but for the food that endures to eternal life, which the Son of Man will give to you. For on him God the Father has set his seal." 28 Then they said to him, "What must we do, to be doing the works of God?" 29 Jesus answered them, "This is the work of God, that you believe in him whom he has sent." 30 So they said to him, "Then what sign do you do, that we may see and believe you? What work do you perform? 31 Our fathers ate the manna in the wilderness; as it is written, 'He gave them bread from heaven to eat.'" 32 Jesus then said to them, "Truly, truly, I say to you, it was not Moses who gave you the bread from heaven,

but my Father gives you the true bread from heaven. [33] For the bread of God is he who comes down from heaven and gives life to the world." [34] They said to him, "Sir, give us this bread always."

[35] Jesus said to them, "I am the bread of life; whoever comes to me shall not hunger, and whoever believes in me shall never thirst. [36] But I said to you that you have seen me and yet do not believe. [37] All that the Father gives me will come to me, and whoever comes to me I will never cast out. [38] For I have come down from heaven, not to do my own will but the will of him who sent me. [39] And this is the will of him who sent me, that I should lose nothing of all that he has given me, but raise it up on the last day. [40] For this is the will of my Father, that everyone who looks on the Son and believes in him should have eternal life, and I will raise him up on the last day."

[47] Truly, truly, I say to you, whoever believes has eternal life. [48] I am the bread of life. [49] Your fathers ate the manna in the wilderness, and they died. [50] This is the bread that comes down from heaven, so that one may eat of it and not die. [51] I am the living bread that came down from heaven. If anyone eats of this bread, he will live forever. And the bread that I will give for the life of the world is my flesh."

____

____

____

____

____

Jesus supernaturally fed the 5,000 through multiplying it in the baskets He's just demonstrated that the spiritual supersedes the physical—and that He can do remarkable things. The Jews who experienced this supernatural work wanted Jesus to perform more supernatural work, but He said that their work was to believe in the Father who sent Him. They said they would believe after Jesus performed another supernatural work, and then they reminded Jesus that their ancestors ate manna in the desert. Jesus responds to that statement by clarifying that the Father gave this manna—it wasn't Moses. He then makes the statement: "'I am' the bread of life." This is about Him.

There is something intuitive about that statement. What does bread bring you? Sustenance, life, nourishment, the ability to live. He is not the temporary bread, but He is eternal, He is fullness for all of life. He has come to give that life, and if you dine on Him, you'll experience life—eternal life.

The beauty of scripture is that He explains exactly what that means. It's more than just a ticket to heaven. He is the bread of life and you need to receive Him— just as you would receive food. He's going to sustain you through His Word. He will give you His Word, which is Him, and it's going to give you life because He is the bread of life.

Upon hearing Jesus say He was the bread of life and later that we should drink of His blood, a number of people following Him took His words literally and left. They exercised their free will, and instead of questioning exactly what He meant or try to understand, they chose not to pursue Him further. Did Jesus chase them down and try to change their minds? No, He did not. Receiving the bread of life is always by invitation. God invites us to follow Him, but we have free will either to choose Him or turn away. After their departure, He turned to His disciples and asked if they, too, wanted to leave. Peter says, "No, we have already chosen you." He pursues this further asking Jesus if what He really meant was that since He is the bread of life, the "I am," that He has the words to life—eternal life. His words to life are what need to be eaten, taken in, absorbed.

John 6:63 says, "It is the Spirit who gives life; the flesh is no help at all. The words that I have spoken to you are spirit and life." In John 17:3, Jesus defines eternal life—not a ticket to heaven, but knowing the Father and knowing the Son. "And this is eternal life, that they know you, the only true God, and Jesus Christ whom you have sent."

The Greek word know is not our typical understanding of knowing— intellectually knowing about—but rather participating in, experiencing, real life. We are called to have this life—the life of God the Father, God the Son, God the Holy Spirit. That's eternal life. How do we get this? Through the bread of life, by eating the words that He speaks. Because that is His life for us. It's Him. When you're abiding in scripture, His Word, you're not just reading history, you are receiving Him—the life of Christ. His words are spirit and life. He is Logos. He is the Word you need to consume. If you're going to eat the bread of life and experience His life, you've got to chew on and digest the Word.

What is the connection between the manna provided every day in the wilderness and Jesus as the bread of life? What are we to do with this bread? When and why?

Read Deuteronomy 8:1–10:

Remember the Lord Your God

8 "The whole commandment that I command you today you shall be careful to do, that you may live and multiply, and go in and possess the land that the LORD swore to give to your fathers. [2] And you shall remember the whole way that the LORD your God has led you these forty years in the wilderness, that he might humble you, testing you to know what was in your heart, whether you would keep his commandments or not. [3] And he humbled you and let you hunger and fed you with manna, which you did not know, nor did your fathers know, that he might make you know that man does not live by bread alone, but man lives by every word[a] that comes from the mouth of the LORD. [4] Your clothing did not wear out on you and your foot did not swell these forty years. [5] Know then in your heart that, as a man disciplines his son, the LORD your God disciplines you. [6] So you shall keep the commandments of the LORD your God by walking in his ways and by fearing him. [7] For the LORD your God is bringing you into a good land, a land of brooks of water, of fountains and springs, flowing out in the valleys and hills, [8] a land of wheat and barley, of vines and fig trees and pomegranates, a land of olive trees and honey, [9] a land in which you will eat bread without scarcity, in which you will lack nothing, a land whose stones are iron, and out of whose hills you can dig copper. [10] And you shall eat and be full, and you shall bless the LORD your God for the good land he has given you.

God reminds the children of those who left Egypt and wandered around in the desert for 40 years. All of their parents died outside of God's will because they refused to be persuaded that what God had to say is true. Because of this choice, they could not enter the Promised Land. During those 40 years, God provided manna every day. He takes this deeper as He describes real food as His word, and how we are to eat these words and live. If you eat these words, you're going to receive His instruction. You'll be led to what He promises, which is to good and to plenty. Best and none better. His promise is spectacular, and you're going to enjoy it to the fullest.

The key is to eat of the bread—who is Him and His words that He speaks to us. If you're going to receive the bread of life, you've got to listen, receive, process, and chew on His Word. It's not intellectual theology, it's personal. It is what is called rhema to you that God is going to speak—that you eat, understand, and be led to the Covenant. Blessed to be a blessing.

What was the purpose of the Passover? Why did God want the Israelites to remember and perform Passover every year? Associated with Passover is the Feast of Tabernacles—what is this? Why do these two feasts go together? How are we then to live these out now as believers?

Read Deuteronomy 16:1–17:

Passover
16 "Observe the month of Abib and keep the Passover to the LORD your God, for in the month of Abib the LORD your God brought you out of Egypt by night. ²And you shall offer the Passover sacrifice to the LORD your God, from the flock or the herd, at the place that the LORD will choose, to make his name dwell there. ³ You shall eat no leavened bread with it. Seven days you shall eat it with unleavened bread, the bread of affliction—for you came out of the land of Egypt in haste—that all the days of your life you may remember the day when you came out of the land of Egypt. ⁴ No leaven shall be seen with you in all your territory for seven days, nor shall any of the flesh that you sacrifice on the evening of the first day remain all night until morning. ⁵ You may not offer the Passover sacrifice within any of your towns that the LORD your God is giving you, ⁶ but at the place that the LORD your God will choose, to make his name dwell in it, there you shall offer the Passover sacrifice, in the evening at sunset, at the time you came out of Egypt. ⁷ And you shall cook it and eat it at the place that

the LORD your God will choose. And in the morning you shall turn and go to your tents. [8] For six days you shall eat unleavened bread, and on the seventh day there shall be a solemn assembly to the LORD your God. You shall do no work on it.

The Feast of Weeks

[9] "You shall count seven weeks. Begin to count the seven weeks from the time the sickle is first put to the standing grain. [10] Then you shall keep the Feast of Weeks to the LORD your God with the tribute of a freewill offering from your hand, which you shall give as the LORD your God blesses you. [11] And you shall rejoice before the LORD your God, you and your son and your daughter, your male servant and your female servant, the Levite who is within your towns, the sojourner, the fatherless, and the widow who are among you, at the place that the LORD your God will choose, to make his name dwell there. [12] You shall remember that you were a slave in Egypt; and you shall be careful to observe these statutes.

The Feast of Booths

[13] "You shall keep the Feast of Booths seven days, when you have gathered in the produce from your threshing floor and your winepress. [14] You shall rejoice in your feast, you and your son and your daughter, your male servant and your female servant, the Levite, the sojourner, the fatherless, and the widow who are within your towns. [15] For seven days you shall keep the feast to the LORD your God at the place that the LORD will choose, because the LORD your God will bless you in all your produce and in all the work of your hands, so that you will be altogether joyful.

[16] "Three times a year all your males shall appear before the LORD your God at the place that he will choose: at the Feast of Unleavened Bread, at the Feast of Weeks, and at the Feast of Booths. They shall not appear before the LORD empty-handed. [17] Every man shall give as he is able, according to the blessing of the LORD your God that he has given you.

Passover was initiated in Egypt where God put to death the firstborn of all those not protected, so that Pharaoh would let Israel depart from slavery. In order for the Israelites not to have their firstborn killed, since the judgment was coming on all in the land, they had to sacrifice lambs, put the blood on their doorposts, and go through the experience of eating the unleavened bread. They did that so they could experience deliverance and protection. God reminds those now willing to go into the Promised to always remember to celebrate Passover each year.

How is Passover to be celebrated? By eating the unleavened bread and drinking the wine. Where is Passover to be celebrated? Where God tells you to go—a place of God's choosing where He puts His name. What's His name? I am.

We need to fully understand this. Passover is joining God in receiving the basis upon which the nation was saved:

- through the blood of sacrifice.

- where He so directs us to follow Him.

- His place where His name is "I am."

After Passover, what celebration followed? The Feast of Tabernacles, which was the celebration of God's provision and abundance. God wanted His children to rejoice and expect the very, very best because of the Passover, which was a step into the supernatural. What initiates this? Eating the bread—His Word, His body, His sacrifice. Jesus expanded on the meaning of this when He was in the upper room before He went to Gethsemane and to the cross.

How did Jesus more fully define the Passover? What then is the purpose of us taking communion regularly? What are we to understand as we take communion regularly? Why?

Read Matthew 26:26–29:

Institution of the Lord's Supper

26 Now as they were eating, Jesus took bread, and after blessing it broke it and gave it to the disciples, and said, "Take, eat; this is my body." 27 And he took a cup, and when he had given thanks he gave it to them, saying, "Drink of it, all of you, 28 for this is my blood of the[a] covenant, which is poured out for many for the forgiveness of sins. 29 I tell you I will not drink again of this fruit of the vine until that day when I drink it new with you in my Father's kingdom."

____

____

____

____

____

Passover is what? Himself. His sacrifice—the giving of His body so that we can have life with Him. Jesus shows the disciples and us: This is Me. You've got to eat My body, My Word, which is My essence, in order to receive the opportunity for life in the Kingdom—life that is spectacular and is a step into the supernatural.

In Corinthians, Paul said to examine yourselves. He did this because they were coming to Passover, to communion with hearts that were not willing to experience all that this means. They were, in fact, careless and did not have hearts to follow Him. However, Jesus didn't say any of that. Yes, it is important to come with a heart to follow because if you don't, then Passover means nothing, but Jesus just said—eat of it and drink of it. Why? Because He is the Passover and a step into the supernatural.

Jesus uses the word remember a number of times. In the Greek, this word is much stronger than to just have a memory of something. The Greek definition is: join Me in what I did when I went to death and was resurrected. Join Me in death to self—your will— and be raised into the supernatural life of God for you. He connects a truth that we read in John 1:14: And the Word (Christ) became flesh and dwelt among us, and we have seen his glory, glory as of the only Son from the Father, full of grace and truth. It is because of this that we are to eat His flesh to receive the fullness of this life—a step into the supernatural.

LESSON 1:
"I AM" THE BREAD OF LIFE

In light of what we are learning about the bread of life, what did Jesus mean when we are to ask for this day, our daily bread? How are we then to receive this daily? Why is this so important?

> **Read Luke 11:1–4:**
>
> The Lord's Prayer
> **11** Now Jesus[a] was praying in a certain place, and when he finished, one of his disciples said to him, "Lord, teach us to pray, as John taught his disciples." [2] And he said to them, "When you pray, say:
>
> "Father, hallowed be your name.
> Your kingdom come.
> [3] Give us each day our daily bread,[b]
> [4] and forgive us our sins,
>   for we ourselves forgive everyone who is indebted to us.
> And lead us not into temptation."

____

____

____

____

____

As Jesus teaches us how to pray, He says we are to ask for what? This day, our daily bread. Who's the bread? Jesus. "I am the bread of life." When is He the bread of life? Today. We are to pray, "Give us this day, our daily bread." In other words, "Father, cause me to be able to eat and chew and receive the daily bread, which is You—given through Your Word." When does that happen? Every day. It's not a Bible study once a week. It's every day. Abide in Him, and let His Word be your daily sustenance. In receiving this daily bread, this life will be best and none better.

The Light of the World:

What does it mean when Jesus says, "He is the Light of the World?" What is the value and purpose of light? What then is important for us to live in this light? Why?

> **Read John 8:12–30:**
>
> I Am the Light of the World
>
> 12 Again Jesus spoke to them, saying, "I am the light of the world. Whoever follows me will not walk in darkness, but will have the light of life." 13 So the Pharisees said to him, "You are bearing witness about yourself; your testimony is not true." 14 Jesus answered, "Even if I do bear witness about myself, my testimony is true, for I know where I came from and where I am going, but you do not know where I come from or where I am going. 15 You judge according to the flesh; I judge no one. 16 Yet even if I do judge, my judgment is true, for it is not I alone who judge, but I and the Father[a] who sent me. 17 In your Law it is written that the testimony of two people is true. 18 I am the one who bears witness about myself, and the Father who sent me bears witness about me." 19 They said to him therefore, "Where is your Father?" Jesus answered, "You know neither me nor my Father. If you knew me, you would know my Father also." 20 These words he spoke in the treasury, as he taught in the temple; but no one arrested him, because his hour had not yet come.
>
> 21 So he said to them again, "I am going away, and you will seek me, and you will die in your sin. Where I am going, you cannot come." 22 So the Jews said, "Will he kill himself, since he says, 'Where I am going, you cannot come'?" 23 He said to them, "You are from below; I am from above. You are of this world; I am not of this world. 24 I told you that you would die in your sins, for unless you believe that I am he you will die in your sins." 25 So they said to him, "Who are you?" Jesus said to them, "Just what I have been telling you from the beginning. 26 I have much to say about you and much to judge, but he who sent me is true, and I declare to the world what I have heard from him." 27 They did not understand that he had been speaking to them about the Father. 28 So Jesus said to them, "When you have lifted up the Son of Man, then you will know that I am he,

> and that I do nothing on my own authority, but speak just as the Father taught me. [29] And he who sent me is with me. He has not left me alone, for I always do the things that are pleasing to him." [30] As he was saying these things, many believed in him.

____

____

____

____

When Jesus says, "I am the light of the world," what exactly does that mean? Why do you need light? So that you don't walk in the dark. In the absence of light, where are you going to be? Walking in the dark. If you are of the world, by definition, where are you? In the dark—walking in darkness.

Jesus knew that none of the Pharisees had a heart to get out of the darkness. This is a dangerous place, especially because if any of them were asked, they would say that they were in the light. This is what they truly believed. Jesus made it clear that was not the case. Why aren't they in the light? Because they're not with Him. They're not receiving Him. Who is the light? The only light is Him. It's not about knowing the Bible or knowing theology. They knew the Bible, and they knew theology, but they didn't know who Jesus was because they were not seeking Him. They were not seeking "I am." They were trying to determine their own light, and in doing so, they were missing the true light.

Jesus further explained that He did nothing except what the Father told Him. The Father spoke to Him, and He followed Him and His Word to Him—just as they are to follow. By following His Word and His will, you pursue the light that takes you out of darkness.

The tabernacle was also called the Tent of Meeting—where the Israelites could meet with and talk with God. In the tabernacle, there was always to be what? How was this to be kept functioning? How does the oil needed for the light to burn relate to us as believers? How are we to operate in the same way? Why?

Read Exodus 27:20–21:

Oil for the Lamp

[20] "You shall command the people of Israel that they bring to you pure beaten olive oil for the light, that a lamp may regularly be set up to burn. [21] In the tent of meeting, outside the veil that is before the testimony, Aaron and his sons shall tend it from evening to morning before the LORD. It shall be a statute forever to be observed throughout their generations by the people of Israel.

____

____

____

____

____

This is symbolic. This is in the tabernacle—in a specific place. The Tent of Meeting, that's where they prayed and burnt incense as an aroma to God and God's glory there.

So, what happened in the Tent of Meeting? The priest met with God—where he had conversation with God. God said that when you are in that place with Him, you'll be in His presence. In this place, they are to make sure there is always what? There is always light. At that point in time, what was necessary for that light to be functioning? They would need a continuous supply of oil for the light to burn.

Let's put this together. Who's the light? Christ. Who's in you? Christ. Who's the Holy Spirit? The oil. We are told not to grieve the Holy Spirit, but rather be filled with the Holy Spirit. Since He is already there, let Him fill you with what? His anointing.

So, if you're in the light, you are not in darkness. If you are walking in the light, what do you know? Direction. You know exactly where to go. There's no questioning or fumbling around. There's no wondering if you are in the right spot. You will see that you are right where He wants you to be. You are in the light, He is the light of the world, and you are letting the Holy Spirit keep that light burning— one step at a time. He is a lamp unto your feet for this step, and the next ones, as well. There are lots of forks in the road, but there is no need to worry because He is the light unto your path.

A key component that must be mentioned is what happens when personal will becomes involved. We tend to think God's got it all set, and we've only been given a blueprint. While God guides us, there are lots of times He is offering invitations to other people along your path to see if they, too, have a heart to follow Him.

For example, after Joshua had conquered Jericho, Ai was the next city to conquer. His men said they could handle this, no problem, and were soundly defeated. Was that God's will? No. He didn't ordain them to get defeated. Joshua reacted to the situation by complaining about how they should have stayed in Egypt. This took place after 40 years of believing God and that His promise was for him to go to the Promised Land. This was the very promise that he was beginning to experience.

God responds by asking Joshua if he remembers what He taught him and then reminds him that he needs to ask Him for guidance each step of the way. Joshua needed to receive the light from Him, but he forgot that step and decided to go on his own. Because he went into darkness, he suffered a consequence. Joshua understood and asked God what his next step should be and what God had to say to him about this. God then tells Joshua that he has sin in the camp. Once Joshua takes care of it, He will lead him to victory in the next city. Joshua needed to seek God's will, just as we are to do the same.

Are you seeking the light step by step or staying in the darkness and experiencing trouble? Come to the light because the light is Him, and He wants it to forever be burning in and for you.

What does Daniel reveal is associated with the light? What does that mean for us? How are we to walk with God in the light to receive these benefits? Why is this so important for us?

Read Daniel 2:20–23:

[20] Daniel answered and said:
"Blessed be the name of God forever and ever,
   to whom belong wisdom and might.
[21] He changes times and seasons;
   he removes kings and sets up kings;
he gives wisdom to the wise
   and knowledge to those who have understanding;
[22] he reveals deep and hidden things;
   he knows what is in the darkness,
   and the light dwells with him.
[23] To you, O God of my fathers,
   I give thanks and praise,
for you have given me wisdom and might,
   and have now made known to me what we asked of you,
   for you have made known to us the king's matter."

Daniel says that God is the light, and light is associated with wisdom. God says He will show you the way and give you understanding of the way. While you're walking in the light, He will tell you secrets. What secrets? He will share behind-the-scenes information that's not available by natural means. As you're seeing things and as you're walking with Him in the light, He will tell you even more profound truths and insights that you can't even imagine. Who gets the privilege of these secrets? Those of us who are in the light. If you're in the darkness, these secrets—this information—is not available to you. You're not going to receive it. God said, "I am the light." Stay in the light, and let Him guide you. Let Him give you wisdom and understanding.

What does light do? What then is important for us as we face the darkness of the world? Why?

Read John 1:4–5:

[4] In him was life,[a] and the life was the light of men. [5] The light shines in the darkness, and the darkness has not overcome it.

Jesus is the light. What does the light do? It shines in the darkness. Darkness doesn't understand it and is unable to overcome it. So, of the two, light or dark, which is more powerful? The light. Because of this truth, you don't have to worry that darkness is going to overwhelm you. God will give you truth. This light gives you the ability to hear, follow, and understand. Why? Because darkness can't overcome it.

Paul describes that Jesus is the light and says that this reflected in Christ's good confession. From the following two verses, what is the good confession? What does that mean for how we live? Why?

Read 1 Timothy 6:13–16:

13 I charge you in the presence of God, who gives life to all things, and of Christ Jesus, who in his testimony before[a] Pontius Pilate made the good confession, 14 to keep the commandment unstained and free from reproach until the appearing of our Lord Jesus Christ, 15 which he will display at the proper time—he who is the blessed and only Sovereign, the King of kings and Lord of lords, 16 who alone has immortality, who dwells in unapproachable light, whom no one has ever seen or can see. To him be honor and eternal dominion. Amen.

____

____

____

____

____

The light is Christ, and Paul describes His good confession, which is another beautiful example of abiding.

Read John 18:19–38:

The High Priest Questions Jesus
19 The high priest then questioned Jesus about his disciples and his teaching. 20 Jesus answered him, "I have spoken openly to the world. I have always taught in synagogues and in the temple, where all Jews come together. I have said nothing in secret. 21 Why do you ask me? Ask those who have heard me what I said to them; they know what I said." 22 When he had said these things, one of the officers standing by struck Jesus with his hand, saying, "Is that

---

how you answer the high priest?"[23] Jesus answered him, "If what I said is wrong, bear witness about the wrong; but if what I said is right, why do you strike me?"[24] Annas then sent him bound to Caiaphas the high priest.

Peter Denies Jesus Again

[25] Now Simon Peter was standing and warming himself. So they said to him, "You also are not one of his disciples, are you?" He denied it and said, "I am not."[26] One of the servants of the high priest, a relative of the man whose ear Peter had cut off, asked, "Did I not see you in the garden with him?"[27] Peter again denied it, and at once a rooster crowed.

Jesus Before Pilate

[28] Then they led Jesus from the house of Caiaphas to the governor's headquarters.[a] It was early morning. They themselves did not enter the governor's headquarters, so that they would not be defiled, but could eat the Passover. [29] So Pilate went outside to them and said, "What accusation do you bring against this man?"[30] They answered him, "If this man were not doing evil, we would not have delivered him over to you."[31] Pilate said to them, "Take him yourselves and judge him by your own law." The Jews said to him, "It is not lawful for us to put anyone to death."[32] This was to fulfill the word that Jesus had spoken to show by what kind of death he was going to die.

My Kingdom Is Not of This World

[33] So Pilate entered his headquarters again and called Jesus and said to him, "Are you the King of the Jews?"[34] Jesus answered, "Do you say this of your own accord, or did others say it to you about me?"[35] Pilate answered, "Am I a Jew? Your own nation and the chief priests have delivered you over to me. What have you done?"[36] Jesus answered, "My kingdom is not of this world. If my kingdom were of this world, my servants would have been fighting, that I might not be delivered over to the Jews. But my kingdom is not from the world."[37] Then Pilate said to him, "So you are a king?" Jesus answered, "You say that I am a king. For this purpose I was born and for this purpose I have come into the world—to bear witness to the truth. Everyone who is of the truth listens to my voice."[38] Pilate said to him, "What is truth?"

After he had said this, he went back outside to the Jews and told them, "I find no guilt in him.

____

____

____

____

____

When Jesus was being questioned by Pilate, He said His Kingdom is not of this world. If His Kingdom were of this world, His servants would fight so that He should not be delivered to the Jews. But His Kingdom is not from here. Pilate then asked Him if He was a king? Based upon Jesus' statement, this would be a natural question. If you say you have a kingdom, are you actually a king? Jesus tells Pilate that He came into the world to become a king, that He should bear witness to the truth. Then, He said that everyone who is of the truth hears His voice.

This is the good confession. He has come to the world. He is the light of the world. He has come to the world that He should, as the light, bear witness to the truth, and everyone who has a heart to receive that truth hears His voice. In other words, light is going to come through Christ speaking the truth so that we followers are led by the light to the truth. Pilate then asks, "What is truth?" After he asked this question, he ended the conversation.

Pilate was engaged in genuine dialogue with Jesus, asking a number of questions. When he concluded the conversation after asking what truth is, he wasn't actually asking the question seeking an answer. He was saying there is no truth—which is why he didn't pursue it any further. When Jesus said that anyone who hears His voice hears the truth, Pilate should have asked Jesus to tell him the truth, or help him understand what truth Jesus wished to reveal to him. Instead, he decided there isn't any truth, and he was not going to pursue this conversation anymore.

What Jesus then did, tells us something about truth:

1. We are called to have a heart to hear His voice. If you're going to stay in the light, you've got to have a heart for truth.

2. If you're going to go to truth, you're going to hear Him speak truth to you. We hear, receive, and continue to process in dialogue with Him.

That is His good confession.

When you come to the light, you are to come to truth. What then is truth, and how do we stay in the light? Why is this so important to how we live?

Read John 3:16–21:

For God So Loved the World

[16] "For God so loved the world,[a] that he gave his only Son, that whoever believes in him should not perish but have eternal life. [17] For God did not send his Son into the world to condemn the world, but in order that the world might be saved through him. [18] Whoever believes in him is not condemned, but whoever does not believe is condemned already, because he has not believed in the name of the only Son of God. [19] And this is the judgment: the light has come into the world, and people loved the darkness rather than the light because their works were evil. [20] For everyone who does wicked things hates the light and does not come to the light, lest his works should be exposed. [21] But whoever does what is true comes to the light, so that it may be clearly seen that his works have been carried out in God."

____

____

____

____

____

If you're going to come to the light, you're always pursuing what? Truth. Seek the truth in everything—every situation, every difficult scenario, every problem, every circumstance. Let Him help you understand the truth. As you get to the truth, you'll stay in the light, and the truth will keep you on the path of God's will, which is best and none better. If you stay in the light, He will bring you super abundance because He can perform the things to have you live it out based on the truth.

I was discipling a young CEO who had left his company and was seeking a new position. I worked with he and his wife to try to define the desires of their heart—what was important to them, what was the truth. He and his wife decided that a certain type of company and a certain culture were important. He only wanted to travel two nights a week, every other week, because they have two children, and he didn't want to be away from his wife and their kids. We spoke of this in great detail and both understood and confirmed that this was their truth.

A short time later, he received a job offer that required traveling four to five nights a week, every week, but the money was doubled. What do you think he said when he received this offer? He believed this was God's answer for giving him a new job—that it was what God wanted. He was seeking God, he was seeking a job, and they were offering him that job. In addition, with all that extra money, he could do so much more with ministry.

When I heard this, I said, "Wait a minute. I thought you were standing in the light; pursuing the light—based on truth. What did you and your wife confirm? Two nights every other week. Why would you violate what you know to be true? God's will and abundance comes by standing in the light and standing on truth—the truth already revealed to you." I urged him to reconsider and asked if his wife also confirmed that this offer is of God. When he said no, I advised him keep processing together what he knew to be true and what he was hearing.

Stay in the light—which always requires faith. Move forward into the truth we know and trust that God will deliver His perfect will, based upon that truth that guides us to His best and none better. If you don't have a heart to stand on the truth, you'll drift away and not experience His best—which likely includes difficulty and hardship.

The CEO reconsidered and decided not to take this offer. Three weeks later, he got another job offer—one that required travel two nights a week, every other week. Not only that, but this also had the same amount of money as the first offer—double what he had made before.

Stay in the light because He is the light. Stay with Him and let His words be spoken to you. He will tell you secrets. Stand on the truth and always have a heart to go to truth; never be afraid of new information because His light will show you the way to the best.

Jesus says, "I'm the bread of life. I'm the light of the world." As we finish this first lesson about the life of Jesus, we are to begin to understand the "I am." The "I am" is everything you need. The "I am" is the bread of life. The "I am" is Passover. The "I am" is the step into the supernatural, the step into the feast of Tabernacles. The "I am" is the light of the world who will tell you secrets and lead you into the very, very best. Stay with Him and live out His life that He promises to deliver to you—which means always going to truth. Darkness will never overcome you, and you'll never be unclear of your path.

LESSON 2:
"I AM" THE DOOR/GATE TO ABUNDANT LIFE

As we continue our course: *The Life of Jesus—I Am,* we're learning the characteristics of Jesus, who is the "I am." "I am" is God—all of God and all that we need for all of life. In Lesson 1, we learned that Jesus is the bread of life and the light of the world. We're supposed to eat Him, chew on Him, digest His Word, and then follow Him into the light, into the truth so that we are never in darkness.

The Gate:

From the following four verses: What are the functions of a gate? How does Jesus fulfill these functions? What are the benefits to us who go through the gate? What does that mean for how we then relate to the gate? Why is this so important for us to understand for the fullness of our life?

> **"I am" is God—all of God and all that we need for all of life."**

Read John 10:7–10:

[7] So Jesus again said to them, "Truly, truly, I say to you, I am the door of the sheep. [8] All who came before me are thieves and robbers, but the sheep did not listen to them. [9] I am the door. If anyone enters by me, he will be saved and will go in and out and find pasture. [10] The thief comes only to steal and kill and destroy. I came that they may have life and have it abundantly.

____

____

____

____

____

Jesus says, "I am the gate." What's a gate? A gate gives entrance and access, but it also provides protection. It allows entrance for those who are supposed to be there and keeps out those who aren't. As the gate, Jesus provides access to what He has come to give us—life; super-abundant life, the beautiful life of God, the Covenant life of God, the blessing. Enter through Him into that place that He is providing for you. He's both the shepherd and the gate, so He will take care of you; but He is also the entrance point. Let's learn what that looks like.

Read Psalm 24:7–10:

7 Lift up your heads, O gates!
And be lifted up, O ancient doors,
that the King of glory may come in.
8 Who is this King of glory?
The Lord, strong and mighty,
the Lord, mighty in battle!
9 Lift up your heads, O gates!
And lift them up, O ancient doors,
that the King of glory may come in.
10 Who is this King of glory?
The Lord of hosts,
he is the King of glory! *Selah*

____

____

____

____

____

Jesus is the gate. Lift up the gates, lift up the doors so that the King may come in. He is both the entrance and the object. If you allow Him to come in and you come in through Him, you will experience Him, who also then comes with you. This is very interesting. Jesus is the gate, but as shepherd and King, He gives you the super abundant life. So, lift up the gates, lift up the doors—lift up—so that the King of glory, who's strong and mighty, can provide you the true experience of the abundant life.

Read Psalm 118:19–20:

19 Open to me the gates of righteousness,
   that I may enter through them
   and give thanks to the LORD.
20 This is the gate of the LORD;
   the righteous shall enter through it.

____

____

____

____

____

Are you righteous? No, but you are righteous in Him, who is righteous. So, open up the gate. Who's the gate? Jesus, and He's righteous. What gives you the ability to enter the gate? The Kingdom of God—righteousness, peace, and joy in the Holy Spirit.

If you are trying to get into the Kingdom by yourself, you can't get there. If you come through the gate of righteousness, as soon as you cross through that gate, you're righteous. How come? Because He's the gate, He is righteous, and His righteousness covers you. There are no other entry points, there is no other way except by stepping through the gate of righteousness.

If you're going to step through the gate of righteousness, what is required on your part? Perfection. How, then, could an imperfect person enter into the Kingdom? Only through the gate who is righteous. How do you do that? By processing truth, believing, and surrendering. The gate of righteousness leads to the Kingdom. He is the righteous one, He is the King. In order to come in through the gate where He will cover you with His righteousness, you have to surrender your will to His—having a heart to follow the King. You cannot push against the gate and enter with your own effort. Even if you know the entrance is through Christ but you are trying to become holy and righteous and good, you still can't come in. Why? Because you are trying to do it on your own. Apart from God, are you righteous? No. Paul addresses this in Romans 7 when he says the harder he tries, the worse it becomes. Who can save him from this awful situation? He is trying, but he just can't get there. The good news is that Jesus is the gate. So, when you come through Him, by surrendering your will to His and having a heart to follow Him, you will enter into and experience the fullness of the Kingdom.

Read Isaiah 26:1–4:

You Keep Him in Perfect Peace
26 In that day this song will be sung in the land of Judah:
"We have a strong city;
  he sets up salvation
  as walls and bulwarks.
² Open the gates,
  that the righteous nation that keeps faith may enter in.
³ You keep him in perfect peace
  whose mind is stayed on you,
  because he trusts in you.
⁴ Trust in the LORD forever,
  for the LORD GOD is an everlasting rock.

____

____

____

____

____

You can enter into the place of righteousness through the gate—through surrender and having a heart to follow. If you do, keep your mind on Him. Be careful about what this means because many believe that means you should be studying the Bible all day long or praying all day long. That is not what it means. What it means is that you have surrendered to His leading, His guiding, His will all the time. If you keep your mind on Him all the time, seeking His way, not your own, this will allow you to go through the gate, into the place of the Kingdom. On the other side of the gate, He will give you perfect peace. He will give you shalom. It's more than just absence of conflict, it's great favor. It's the abundant life. In the English this says: He will give you perfect peace. In the Hebrew, this says: Peace, peace—shalom, shalom. A double portion. It will be so much that you can't handle it all. All you have to do is what? Come on in. Just come on in, and He will keep you there and give you great favor.

As we seek God's will, we are to listen, watch, and wait. The waiting is at the gate. What happened at the gate and thus, what does this mean to wait there? For what are we waiting? If we wait, what will be given? Why is this so critical to live out our life in Christ?

Read Proverbs 8:32–35:

32 "And now, O sons, listen to me:
   blessed are those who keep my ways.
33 Hear instruction and be wise,
   and do not neglect it.
34 Blessed is the one who listens to me,
   watching daily at my gates,
   waiting beside my doors.
35 For whoever finds me finds life
   and obtains favor from the LORD,

LESSON 2:
"I AM" THE DOOR/GATE TO ABUNDANT LIFE

Blessed are you when you seek wisdom. The key to this blessing is what? Listen to His instruction. He puts three things together here:

1. Listen to the Bread of Life. Listen to what He has to say.

2. Watch for the truth—the light. What do you observe as the truth? Walk into the truth. You will see what God shows you next.

3. Wait at the gate. He's at the gate.

What happens at the gate? In Israel, there is entrance in and out of the city at the gate. There, the elders of the town, who were considered wise and helpful for determining God's will, would gather at the gate. The people would come to the gate and ask: Could you assist me? Could you help me with this decision? Could you help us process this? The people would then wait at the gate until they received an answer. They were not going to move forward until they knew for certain which way to go.

What are you waiting for if you are sitting at the Gate of Christ? You are waiting to find God's will. How would you do this? By listening, watching, and waiting. The waiting is the hardest part. How come? Because you want the answer now, but sometimes with God's answer there is a timing issue. There might be something else He wants to show you before you get to the answer that you are seeking. Trusting Him requires patience. The pressure you feel usually stems from your personal drive or need to receive an immediate answer. Oftentimes, if you haven't received your answer as quickly as you'd like, you start looking for plan B. Scriptures tell you to wait at the gate until the gate itself, Christ, gives you the answer that you need.

Be persistent in your listening, watching, waiting. Stay there until you understand His will. The reason you are even able to be at the gate is because He's invited you to join Him and has provided the way for you to join Him—His righteousness. Stand in His righteousness before Him and have a conversation with a heart for truth. Receive what He has to say at the gate as He is the entrance, the protector, and the one who can give you the answer.

The good shepherd:

What does a good shepherd do? What is crucial for us as sheep then to follow the good shepherd? What does that mean as to how we walk with God? Why is this so important for us to learn and experience?

Read John 10:1–5; 1–18; 25–30:

I Am the Good Shepherd

10 "Truly, truly, I say to you, he who does not enter the sheepfold by the door but climbs in by another way, that man is a thief and a robber. [2] But he who enters by the door is the shepherd of the sheep. [3] To him the gatekeeper opens. The sheep hear his voice, and he calls his own sheep by name and leads them out. [4] When he has brought out all his own, he goes before them, and the sheep follow him, for they know his voice. [5] A stranger they will not follow, but they will flee from him, for they do not know the voice of strangers."

I Am the Good Shepherd

10 "Truly, truly, I say to you, he who does not enter the sheepfold by the door but climbs in by another way, that man is a thief and a robber. [2] But he who enters by the door is the shepherd of the sheep. [3] To him the gatekeeper opens. The sheep hear his voice, and he calls his own sheep by name and leads them out. [4] When he has brought out all his own, he goes before them, and the sheep follow him, for they know his voice. [5] A stranger they will not follow, but they will flee from him, for they do not know the voice of strangers." [6] This figure of speech Jesus used with them, but they did not understand what he was saying to them.

[7] So Jesus again said to them, "Truly, truly, I say to you, I am the door of the sheep. [8] All who came before me are thieves and robbers, but the sheep did not listen to them. [9] I am the door. If anyone enters by me, he will be saved and will go in and out and find pasture. [10] The thief comes only to steal and kill and destroy. I came that they may have life and have it abundantly. [11] I am the good shepherd. The good shepherd lays down his life for the sheep. [12] He who is a hired hand and not a shepherd, who does not own the sheep, sees the wolf coming and leaves the sheep and flees, and the wolf snatches them and scatters them. [13] He flees because he is a hired hand and cares nothing

for the sheep. [14] I am the good shepherd. I know my own and my own know me, [15] just as the Father knows me and I know the Father; and I lay down my life for the sheep. [16] And I have other sheep that are not of this fold. I must bring them also, and they will listen to my voice. So there will be one flock, one shepherd. [17] For this reason the Father loves me, because I lay down my life that I may take it up again. [18] No one takes it from me, but I lay it down of my own accord. I have authority to lay it down, and I have authority

[25] Jesus answered them, "I told you, and you do not believe. The works that I do in my Father's name bear witness about me, [26] but you do not believe because you are not among my sheep. [27] My sheep hear my voice, and I know them, and they follow me. [28] I give them eternal life, and they will never perish, and no one will snatch them out of my hand. [29] My Father, who has given them to me,[a] is greater than all, and no one is able to snatch them out of the Father's hand. [30] I and the Father are one."

____

____

____

____

What kind of a shepherd is He? He is a good shepherd. What is a good shepherd? One who takes care of the sheep. Jesus describes this in John 10 saying, "I stay with you. I never walk away from you. I'm always there with you to take care of you and protect you." His heart is that He cares deeply and loves His sheep. He knows everything about His sheep, which means He knows everything about you, and His will for you is absolute. He will guide you and lead you as a good shepherd. He also says His sheep—if they are truly His sheep—will hear His voice.

When the shepherd speaks, the sheep hear His voice. He is the bread of life, He is the Word, and He is our shepherd who speaks to us and guides us. When we hear His voice, we pay attention because we know it is Him, not the voice of a stranger. Because we know Him and are acquainted with His voice, the difference will be clear and there will be no confusion.

How will you know the voice of Christ versus the voice of the enemy or your own voice telling you what you want to hear? Stay in His presence and listen to His voice.

When babies are only a few months old, they already know their parents' voices. When their mom or dad speaks, a baby responds by following the voice and looking for them. Why is this? Because the baby has been with them and has learned to hear and recognize their voices. When strangers enter the room and say the same words, do babies respond the same way? No, they only respond to the voice they know, the voice they are familiar with, the voice they are hearing continually.

Jesus tells us to learn to recognize the voice of God as He is always speaking. We are to enjoy learning to listen and hear that voice. As a body, we can help each other with this process by asking questions, asking if others are hearing the same thing, if others can provide confirmation. Did you hear what God said? Did you hear that? Did you see that? Did you understand that?

In our retreats, we do an exercise where we go to a private place with our spouse and ask the Father what He has to say about any issues currently on our heart. We then write down what we hear. We are not to try to understand or interpret anything, we are simply to write down everything that we hear. After we did the exercise, we came back together and one person said he heard nothing, not one thing. When we dug deeper, he said he did hear something, but he interpreted it as nothing significant. He dismissed what he heard thinking it was probably his own voice he was hearing. In truth, he actually heard God's voice, but he only realized that when he processed it further with us.

Hearing the voice of God takes practice, but the more you practice, the easier it becomes. With a baby, it's not complicated or confusing. They don't analyze everything. They simply respond to the voice they are familiar with. God's sheep hear His voice, and they know His name. God knows your name, too. When the sheep hear God's voice, they follow. They follow their Shepherd who is leading them down the best possible path to a super-abundant life.

Christ makes another remarkable statement when He says that not only is He the good shepherd, leading you to goodness—He is going to give you the privilege of being able to stay there because He is going to lay down His life for you. Not only is He the shepherd, but He is also the sacrificial lamb. He is both, and He will allow you to have this abundant life with Him. He then says this will be His choice, and nobody, not even the Father is going to help Him out of the process of laying down His life. It's something He has to work through. When did He do that? In the Garden of Gethsemane. He knew it was going to be a battle of the will, to overcome self, which was what caused the world to be handed over to Satan. This was the result when Adam and Eve became sinful with a sin nature due to their disobedience.

Jesus ended His description of the good shepherd in John 10:30 when He said, "I and the Father are one." Jesus does nothing except what the Father speaks and does for Him to follow—including giving Him the strength to follow. However, when it comes to laying down His life for us, the sheep, the Father is not going to help Him. He had to overcome the self. When He went to Gethsemane, He goes in and battles for about an hour or so. He walks out and says, "Not My will be done, but Yours." How come He went back in? Because it wasn't finished. It was in His mind, but it wasn't in his heart—He had not fully surrendered yet, and He knew it. The Father didn't step in and say that He would finish it for Jesus because Jesus had to battle this through to victory.

Paul says in Romans 5 that by one man, sin entered the world through the exercise of the self in disobedience to the Father—but, by another man, Jesus, the will—the self—was conquered, and through obedience gained this life back. When Jesus went into the garden a second time, He had the same result. The third time, it got so intense He sweat blood because He struggled through the release of the self-will to the Father's will of laying down His life. He exits the garden with complete surrender and has no further issue of marching to the cross to lay down His life for us, the sheep. Jesus is the true Good Shepherd.

From the following two verses: The Lord is MY shepherd. The "my" means it is personal. Thus, what are all the promises given to you personally from the shepherd? What do each of the promises mean? How then shall we live out this life as sheep under the leadership of the Shepherd? Why is this so important for us?

Read Psalm 23:1–6:

The LORD Is My Shepherd
A Psalm of David.
23 The LORD is my shepherd; I shall not want.
²   He makes me lie down in green pastures.
He leads me beside still waters.[a]
³   He restores my soul.
He leads me in paths of righteousness[b]
   for his name's sake.

> [4] Even though I walk through the valley of the shadow of death,[c]
>   I will fear no evil,
> for you are with me;
>   your rod and your staff,
>   they comfort me.
> [5] You prepare a table before me
>   in the presence of my enemies;
> you anoint my head with oil;
>   my cup overflows.
> [6] Surely[d] goodness and mercy[e] shall follow me
>   all the days of my life,
> and I shall dwell[f] in the house of the LORD
>   forever.[g]

____

____

____

____

____

The Lord is my shepherd. He's become your personal shepherd. You shall not want as He will be your provider. He will make you lie down—to refresh you; to give you a very peaceful, joyful life. The busyness that you think is a badge of honor is actually the opposite of the abundant, peaceful life available to you through being led by "My Shepherd." When you are not experiencing rest and peace, it is because you've stopped following Him. However, God is going to help you—He will make you to lie down and be refreshed by still waters. Living in the world, there will always be trouble. God will not take you out of the trouble, but He will get you through it. He will get you to a place where you enjoy the life He has for you even in the middle of your problems.

In addition, He will prepare a feast—a spectacular feast—for you. Your troubles will not bother you since you will be enjoying all that He will provide. Then surely—absolutely—goodness and mercy shall follow you all the days of your life.

The word *mercy* in the Hebrew is "Covenant loyalty." God is loyal to the Covenant—always. He will give you the Covenant, which means you are blessed to be a blessing. The shepherd is always leading you to what? Abundant life of the Covenant. His path is for you to be blessed and to be a blessing. He knows you're going to have trouble, but He is going to take care of it. If you have a heart to hear His voice and follow Him as your good shepherd, you'll receive the Covenant.

Read Psalm 28:6–9:

[6] Blessed be the LORD!
   For he has heard the voice of my pleas for mercy.
[7] The LORD is my strength and my shield;
   in him my heart trusts, and I am helped;
my heart exults,
   and with my song I give thanks to him.
[8] The LORD is the strength of his people;[a]
   he is the saving refuge of his anointed.
[9] Oh, save your people and bless your heritage!
   Be their shepherd and carry them forever.

____

____

____

____

____

What are the characteristics of the good shepherd?

- He is for us.

- He protects us.

- He gives us strength.

- He gives us the super-abundant life.

- He brings us salvation.

What is salvation? It is wholeness and deliverance. It's the fullness of the life of God. He said the shepherd brings you the fullness of the life of God. He's the good shepherd, and what does the good shepherd do? He takes care of the sheep, He lays down His life for His sheep—each of us. Why does He do this? So that you can experience the super-abundant life.

The good shepherd is not a temporary position. He doesn't leave us to fail, go back to self, and figure things out on our own. No, He is always the good shepherd who is leading us to the Covenant. Psalm 23 makes it clear that you're going to be in the presence of the enemy and you're going to have trouble, but He is the good shepherd, and He will take care of you. He is both the entrance— the gate—to allow you to be His sheep, and He is the shepherd who takes care of you.

"I am" the resurrection.

When Jesus calls Himself the resurrection, what does that mean? What are the characteristics of the resurrection? What is required on our part to receive these characteristics in our life? Why is this so important?

Read John 11:17–27; 38–44:

I Am the Resurrection and the Life

[17] Now when Jesus came, he found that Lazarus had already been in the tomb four days. [18] Bethany was near Jerusalem, about two miles[a] off, [19] and many of the Jews had come to Martha and Mary to console them concerning their brother. [20] So when Martha heard that Jesus was coming, she went and met him, but Mary remained seated in the house. [21] Martha said to Jesus, "Lord, if you had been here, my brother would not have died. [22] But even now I know that whatever you ask from God, God will give you." [23] Jesus said to her, "Your brother will rise again." [24] Martha said to him, "I know that he will rise again in the resurrection on the last day." [25] Jesus said to her, "I am the resurrection and the life.[b] Whoever believes in me, though he die, yet shall he live, [26] and everyone who lives and believes in me shall never die. Do you believe this?" [27] She said to him, "Yes, Lord; I believe that you are the Christ, the Son of God, who is coming into the world."

Jesus Raises Lazarus

[38] Then Jesus, deeply moved again, came to the tomb. It was a cave, and a stone lay against it. [39] Jesus said, "Take away the stone." Martha, the sister of the dead man, said to him, "Lord, by this time there will be an odor, for he has been dead four days." [40] Jesus said to her, "Did I not tell you that if you believed you would see the glory of God?" [41] So they took away the stone. And Jesus lifted up his eyes and said, "Father, I thank you that you have heard me. [42] I knew that you always hear me, but I said this on account of the people standing around, that they may believe that you sent me." [43] When he had said these things, he cried out with a loud voice, "Lazarus, come out." [44] The man who had died came out, his hands and feet bound with linen strips, and his face wrapped with a cloth. Jesus said to them, "Unbind him, and let him go."

Mary, Martha, and Lazarus lived in Bethany. As you may recall, in Luke 10:38–42, Jesus was with Mary and Martha. Martha was busy serving Him while Mary sat at His feet and listened to Him speak. Martha wasn't happy about this and asked Jesus to tell Mary to help her. Instead, Jesus told Martha that while she is troubled and distracted and seeking to please herself by doing all of the things she thinks will please Him, Mary is doing the right thing. Martha never asked Jesus what He wanted her to do, and Mary has chosen the better thing which was to be with Him, listening to His voice, and enjoying fellowship with Him.

In this current situation, Lazarus is sick. They send for Jesus asking if He would come and heal him. He agreed but He purposely didn't go right away. Martha was frustrated that Jesus didn't immediately come to Lazarus' aid, but Mary, the one who previously sat at Jesus' feet, was so mad that she refused to come out and talk

This is a profound lesson of our relationship with Christ—it's not a permanent thing. The relationship is dependent on your heart at the moment and is a choice we need to make every day, every moment—to abide and remain in the Vine.

While Mary refuses to talk to Him, Martha goes out and tells Jesus that if He had been here, she knows that He could have healed her brother. But, since Jesus didn't come as quickly as she wanted, now Lazarus was dead. Jesus responds by telling her that he'll be resurrected. This did nothing to calm her frustration. She knew what was supposed to happen at the very end. She had spent enough time with Jesus and knew a bit about eschatology—the part of theology concerned with death, judgment, and the final destiny of the soul and of humankind. But, He corrects her and says that He is the resurrection and the life.

We know that Jesus was resurrected, and we tend to think of resurrection as an event. Yes, He was resurrected, but this goes way beyond that. When He says He is the resurrection, He is saying that He is the rising from death to life. He is the death to life. If you're with Him, He is going to take what's dead, and it's going to become alive again. In addition, it's going to become super abundant.

He is the life of the resurrection. Why? Because He is the resurrection, and He is the life. When He asks Martha if she believes it, she is unsure. When He orders the stone to be rolled away, she reminds Him that Lazarus has been dead for four days, and there will be a strong odor. Jesus says, "Martha, didn't I tell you that if you believe—that I am the resurrection and the life—that you would see the glory of God?" Jesus then puts His power on full display by resurrecting Lazarus. In doing this, He was physically demonstrating that He had the power. All He said was rise. That's it—the resurrection was performed through the power of the Word from who? The bread of life.

To summarize, a sheep follows the shepherd. Jesus is the shepherd. Jesus is the resurrection and the life. Where is Jesus in the resurrection? Where is the power in the resurrection? Who can change death to life? Jesus. Our role is simply to follow Him. When He says to deny self, take up the cross, and follow Him, to where are we following Him? Into the life. Why? Because He is the resurrection. He isn't trying to give you only a portion of the life, He is the life, and He will give you the resurrected life—the powerful life, because that's who He is—the "I am."

We understand the sacrifice that Christ fulfilled at the cross to give us the opportunity to have a relationship with Him. What is the significance of Him having risen? What does that mean for us? Why is this so important to our life?

Read Matthew 28:1–8:

The Resurrection

28 Now after the Sabbath, toward the dawn of the first day of the week, Mary Magdalene and the other Mary went to see the tomb. [2] And behold, there was a great earthquake, for an angel of the Lord descended from heaven and came and rolled back the stone and sat on it. [3] His appearance was like lightning, and his clothing white as snow. [4] And for fear of him the guards trembled and became like dead men. [5] But the angel said to the women, "Do not be afraid, for I know that you seek Jesus who was crucified. [6] He is not here, for he has risen, as he said. Come, see the place where he[a] lay. [7] Then go quickly and tell his disciples that he has risen from the dead, and behold, he is going before you to Galilee; there you will see him. See, I have told you." [8] So they departed quickly from the tomb with fear and great joy, and ran to tell his disciples.

When Jesus died at the cross, what did He do? He sacrificed Himself to take on the penalty for our sin. He stood in our place, which is called propitiation of sin. At the cross, He went to death, becoming the sacrifice for each of us. This sacrifice had to be perfect, but because of our sin nature, through the disobedience of Adam and Eve, we could not be perfect and thus were separated from Him. So, with His death upon the cross, He again gives us the opportunity to have a relationship with Him. Why? Resurrection. We were dead, and the resurrection brings death to life. It was not only the death and the sacrifice, it was the resurrection from the death. He physically was present after His death because of the resurrection. He actually was here.

Why is this so critical that it wasn't just spiritual? Because He demonstrated the full power of resurrection—body, soul, and spirit. The resurrection life brought full restoration from full death, into completeness. It wasn't just spiritual life back to heaven. He was dead physically, and now He's alive physically. This is death to life. He, the "I am," is the resurrection. He is the life—death to life. As we come to understand this, we also understand that we, too, have the opportunity to go from death to life.

We are raised with Christ. What does that mean? What are the four things that Christ fulfilled at His death and resurrection? How then are we to live given that these things have been fulfilled? Why is this so important for us?

Read Colossians 2:11–15:

[11] In him also you were circumcised with a circumcision made without hands, by putting off the body of the flesh, by the circumcision of Christ, [12] having been buried with him in baptism, in which you were also raised with him through faith in the powerful working of God, who raised him from the dead. [13] And you, who were dead in your trespasses and the uncircumcision of your flesh, God made alive together with him, having forgiven us all our trespasses, [14] by canceling the record of debt that stood against us with its legal demands. This he set aside, nailing it to the cross. [15] He disarmed the rulers and authorities[a] and put them to open shame, by triumphing over them in him.[b]

Because Jesus is the resurrection and the life, what's available to you? The same thing, which is for you to join Him by going from death to life. The death of what? Self—then being raised again into the newness of life from death. He says He will bring you with Him into that place. When you're following Him, you're following Him in the resurrection, and you're with Him in that resurrection. What did resurrection do?

1. Provided forgiveness. He forgives you. He forgives all of your sin—past, present, and future. He took care of that, so there's no condemnation. You are forgiven.

2. Fulfilled the requirement for perfection. He took away the requirement that was against you and nailed to the cross. What's the requirement? Perfection. Apart from God, is it possible to obtain perfection? No, so He removed that requirement.

3. He disarmed the powers of the principalities. He took it away. Where does the power of the enemy have zero effect? When you're in Christ, who is the resurrection, Satan has been disarmed and made powerless.

4. Jesus triumphed over Satan. Where has the victory been won? In the resurrection. He urges us to deny self and come to the gate.

Have a heart to go into the Kingdom through His righteousness because He took away the requirement. You can't get in there by yourself. You can only live there by accepting and believing Him and what He did. Once you are through the gate, follow Him in the resurrection where the enemy can't harm you. Jesus brought you into a place where He can take things that are dead, things that aren't working, and make them alive. Not only are they alive, but they are living a resurrected life, a super-abundant life, a supernatural life.

How did the disciples bear witness to the resurrection? How is this different from just speaking about the truth of the resurrection? How then are we to bear witness to the resurrection? Why is this so important?

Read Acts 4:32–33:

They Had Everything in Common

[32] Now the full number of those who believed were of one heart and soul, and no one said that any of the things that belonged to him was his own, but they had everything in common. [33] And with great power the apostles were giving their testimony to the resurrection of the Lord Jesus, and great grace was upon them all.

____

____

____

____

____

These are simple verses with great power. The disciples bore witness to the resurrection. They didn't talk about the resurrection in terms of how Jesus rose from the dead. Instead, they demonstrated the life of the resurrection. How? By performing supernatural stuff. The life of the resurrection is to be a life of the supernatural. It's remarkable. If you are living in the resurrection, bear witness to the supernatural events taking place in your life. You are not simply maneuvering through the natural, you are actually bearing witness to the resurrection life through resurrection power which changes real circumstances.

As we bear witness to the resurrection, what are the benefits to us? How are these benefits given to us? Why is this so important to how we live this life of Christ?

Read 1 Peter 1:1–12:

Greeting

1 Peter, an apostle of Jesus Christ,
To those who are elect exiles of the Dispersion in Pontus, Galatia, Cappadocia, Asia, and Bithynia, [2] according to the foreknowledge of God the Father, in the sanctification of the Spirit, for obedience to Jesus Christ and for sprinkling with his blood:

May grace and peace be multiplied to you.

Born Again to a Living Hope
[3] Blessed be the God and Father of our Lord Jesus Christ! According to his great mercy, he has caused us to be born again to a living hope through the resurrection of Jesus Christ from the dead, [4] to an inheritance that is imperishable, undefiled, and unfading, kept in heaven for you, [5] who by God's power are being guarded through faith for a salvation ready to be revealed in the last time. [6] In this you rejoice, though now for a little while, if necessary, you have been grieved by various trials, [7] so that the tested genuineness of your faith—more precious than gold that perishes though it is tested by fire—may be found to result in praise and glory and honor at the revelation of Jesus Christ. [8] Though you have not seen him, you love him. Though you do not now see him, you believe in him and rejoice with joy that is inexpressible and filled with glory, [9] obtaining the outcome of your faith, the salvation of your souls. [10] Concerning this salvation, the prophets who prophesied about the grace that was to be yours searched and inquired carefully, [11] inquiring what person or time[a] the Spirit of Christ in them was indicating when he predicted the sufferings of Christ and the subsequent glories. [12] It was revealed to them that they were serving not themselves but you, in the things that have now been announced to you through those who preached the good news to you by the Holy Spirit sent from heaven, things into which angels long to look.

____

____

____

____

____

When God says He is going to transfer you into His life so that you may participate in the resurrection, what does this mean? It means that you have an inheritance that doesn't fade away—it is incorruptible, and it is reserved and laid out for you.

Consider the simplicity of what He's saying. You're in the world—a place where you will experience trouble—and He places you with Him in the resurrection. Do you believe that you're in the resurrection. What about all this trouble? What's going to happen with that? God is going to take care of it. He is going to resolve it. Why? Because you're in the resurrection. This means you are in the fullness of the resurrection, receiving its absolute power, might, and resolution. This is why He said it's incorruptible. It's absolute. It's the full power of God.

Do you believe it? The way to believe it is to stay in the resurrection, but when things don't go as quickly as you'd like or the way that you would like, you are constantly tempted to try to find resolution on your own. This is when you go back to death. When Jesus talks about putting to death the Spirit or about grieving the Spirit, it is because you walked away from the life of the resurrection and back into death. What is the remedy when you have walked away? It is to come back to the gate, surrender your will, and return to living in the resurrection. Choose daily to live in the resurrection. In Romans 6, God describes this great progression of the resurrection.

To live the life of the resurrection, it is necessary for us to walk with Him and receive all these benefits. Following the progression described here, what has Christ done to give us this opportunity, and how are we to respond to this? What is the reason we must respond this way? What are the benefits of responding this way?

Read Romans 6:1–7; 18, 22:

Dead to Sin, Alive to God

6 What shall we say then? Are we to continue in sin that grace may abound? [2] By no means! How can we who died to sin still live in it? [3] Do you not know that all of us who have been baptized into Christ Jesus were baptized into his death? [4] We were buried therefore with him by baptism into death, in order that, just as Christ was raised from the dead by the glory of the Father, we too might walk in newness of life.

[5] For if we have been united with him in a death like his, we shall certainly be united with him in a resurrection like his. [6] We know that our old self[a] was crucified with him in order that the body of sin might be brought to nothing, so that we would no longer be enslaved to sin. [7] For one who has died has been set free[b] from sin.

[18] and, having been set free from sin, have become slaves of righteousness.

[22] But now that you have been set free from sin and have become slaves of God, the fruit you get leads to sanctification and its end, eternal life.

Your invitation is to go to death with Him. What comes after this? Living with Him in the resurrection. The purpose of going to death of self is to get to the resurrection life. Is it possible to die to self only once and live in the resurrection permanently? No. How often do we need to die to self? All the time. Many people misinterpret this, believing that when you surrender to God's will, whatever happens, happens. If this is your mindset, unfortunately, you have never actually surrendered. If you have surrendered your will to His, you are living in the resurrection where amazing, supernatural things will take place. Rather than telling God to do whatever He's going to do about any given situation, ask Him what He has to say about this. Then, follow Him and experience all His resurrection power.

It is not a passive surrender—*God, I surrender.* It is more than that. It's surrendering to the path of God that is in the resurrection. In verse 7, he said that sin and death have been taken care of. They were taken care of by the Spirit. Past tense. If that is the case, why is sin still a problem? Go to verse 18.

Do you recall who the gate of righteousness is? Jesus. Who's the shepherd? Jesus. If you are going to experience this, you have to become a slave to Jesus. What does the word *slave* mean? It means being a servant. It means you're wholly invested in Him. Your life is surrendered to Him completely. If you don't follow completely, you automatically go back to self where you've also chosen to go to death from the resurrection. Living in the resurrection is a continuous choice to surrender to Him, to become His slave, and to walk with Him.

In verse 22, He finishes the progression. In John 17:3, we read how Jesus defined everlasting life as knowing Him and experiencing Him. If you understand that you've joined Him in the resurrection, you became His slave. The end result is living with Him in the resurrected life—where you will experience holiness, bounty, abundant life, resolution. You'll see the result when you're there. If you are experiencing that power, you are living with Him in the resurrected life. If you're constantly struggling, you're probably in the flesh. You've likely stopped short of getting to the resurrection because you haven't gotten through the gate. The fruit of being a slave and living in the resurrection is holiness—experiencing the full life of God now.

LESSON 2:
"I AM" THE RESURRECTION AND THE LIFE

As we live in the resurrection, what is God's good work in and for us? What then shall we expect our life to experience? When? Why?

> **Read Hebrews 13:20–21:**
>
> Benediction
> [20] Now may the God of peace who brought again from the dead our Lord Jesus, the great shepherd of the sheep, by the blood of the eternal covenant, [21]equip you with everything good that you may do his will, working in us[a] that which is pleasing in his sight, through Jesus Christ, to whom be glory forever and ever. Amen.

____

____

____

____

____

If you follow the resurrection, the shepherd, and the gate, you will experience the eternal Covenant—the life of blessing and goodness that He has planned for you, His good work. Christ says His good work will always bring you resurrected life. Why? Because He is the "I am" — "I am the resurrection." He can't be anything else. He's not the resurrection only on certain occasions or every once in a while, He is the resurrection. He is the power. He is the abundant life.

We tend to define abundance strictly as financial. Yes, it is financial freedom, but it's all of the resurrection life—it's pleasantness, it's resolution, it's experiencing joy in relationships. It's righteousness, peace, and joy in the Holy Spirit—the Kingdom of the resurrection. The blessings are vast because the resurrection is just as vast. Jesus says, "I am the resurrection." This is for always and for everything in your life.

As we complete this lesson, there is so much beauty in how He describes the fullness of His life: He's the gate, He's the shepherd, and He's the resurrection. All of that is for our good so we can experience the power of this life, the might of this life. Enter through His righteousness, and experience all that He has for you as a good shepherd. Recognize the power because He is the resurrection. Experience that beautiful supernatural work that He can do for you because you're with Him. Enter through Him, the gate, by surrendering and letting His righteousness cover you so you can live this life of the resurrection.

LESSON 3:
"I AM" THE WAY, THE TRUTH, AND THE LIFE

As we continue this course: *The Life of Jesus—I Am*, we should now understood the essence of what this means. When Jesus was asked, "Who are you?" He said, "I am the 'I am,'" which means He is everything. He is all of God—the nature of God, the life of God, the power of God. We've also learned that this includes different characteristics: "I am" the bread of life. "I am" the light of the world. "I am" the gate. "I am" the good shepherd. "I am" the resurrection and the life. Because of His unbelievable power and nature, He doesn't change. The "I am" is always the same and always there for us. Our role is to live with Him in the resurrection, which is coming through the gate, experiencing the life of the good shepherd, eating the body of the bread—His Word—and then experiencing the opportunity to go to truth and be in the light. In doing this, we live the promised abundant life.

The Way, The Truth, and the Life:

What does it mean that Jesus is the way? In order for us to walk in His way, what must we pursue and experience? What does that mean for how we live?

> "When Jesus was asked, 'Who are you?' He said, "I am the 'I am,'" which means He is everything. He is all of God—the nature of God, the life of God, the power of God."

Read John 14:6–14:

[6] Jesus said to him, "I am the way, and the truth, and the life. No one comes to the Father except through me. [7] If you had known me, you would have known my Father also.[a] From now on you do know him and have seen him."

[8] Philip said to him, "Lord, show us the Father, and it is enough for us." [9] Jesus said to him, "Have I been with you so long, and you still do not know me, Philip? Whoever has seen me has seen the Father. How can you say, 'Show us the Father'? [10] Do you not believe that I am in the Father and the Father is in me? The words that I say to you I do not speak

> on my own authority, but the Father who dwells in me does his works. [11] Believe me that I am in the Father and the Father is in me, or else believe on account of the works themselves.
>
> [12] "Truly, truly, I say to you, whoever believes in me will also do the works that I do; and greater works than these will he do, because I am going to the Father. [13] Whatever you ask in my name, this I will do, that the Father may be glorified in the Son. [14] If you ask me[b] anything in my name, I will do it.

____

____

____

____

____

We've been learning that His name is "I am." As you receive the authority of the "I am" and live in the resurrection, you will start to participate and live out the resurrection in your own life. It will involve you. He says that in order to believe this, you will need to understand that the work and the life of the Father is in Him, just as He is in the Father—the "I am." Thus, you're seeing the Father when you see Him.

He then said: If that's hard for you to believe, then believe the miracles which you see and cannot deny. It's not thinking about the life of God, it's experiencing the life of God. You can experience the miracles. Why? Because "I am the way, the truth, and the life—the 'I am.'" We've learned that: "I am" the light of the world—the truth. "I am" the life of the resurrection—the life. "I am" the good shepherd—brings life. He then adds this one more element of it. "I am" the way to this life. If He's the way, what would be important for each of us? To be with Him—be with Him on His way. It's not Him blessing your way. If you are going to experience this life, you're going to have to be with Him on His way—which will become your way. His way is geared toward you personally, and on this path, you will experience the miraculous works of the Father.

If Jesus is the way, the truth, and the life, what is important then for how God guides us? What must our heart be? If we fulfill this requirement, what will the benefits be on the way? What do these mean for our everyday life? Why?

Read Psalm 25:1–15:

Teach Me Your Paths

[a] Of David.

25 To you, O LORD, I lift up my soul.
2 O my God, in you I trust;
   let me not be put to shame;
   let not my enemies exult over me.
3 Indeed, none who wait for you shall be put to shame;
   they shall be ashamed who are wantonly treacherous.
4 Make me to know your ways, O LORD;
   teach me your paths.
5 Lead me in your truth and teach me,
   for you are the God of my salvation;
   for you I wait all the day long.
6 Remember your mercy, O LORD, and your steadfast love,
   for they have been from of old.
7 Remember not the sins of my youth or my transgressions;
   according to your steadfast love remember me,
   for the sake of your goodness, O LORD!
8 Good and upright is the LORD;
   therefore he instructs sinners in the way.
9 He leads the humble in what is right,
   and teaches the humble his way.
10 All the paths of the LORD are steadfast love and faithfulness,
   for those who keep his covenant and his testimonies.
11 For your name's sake, O LORD,
   pardon my guilt, for it is great.
12 Who is the man who fears the LORD?
   Him will he instruct in the way that he should choose.

> [13] His soul shall abide in well-being,
>   and his offspring shall inherit the land.
> [14] The friendship[b] of the LORD is for those who fear him,
>   and he makes known to them his covenant.
> [15] My eyes are ever toward the LORD,
>   for he will pluck my feet out of the net.

____

____

____

____

____

We are to have a heart to learn to walk in God's way. He describes it as truth. "I am" the light of the world and will lead you to truth. This begins with His Covenant loyalty, which in English is described as steadfast love. God is loyal to His Covenant—blessing you to make you a blessing—which is absolute for His way. Why? Because He is the good shepherd. Your role is to be humble, follow Him, and enjoy living in righteousness, which is releasing the burden of sin nature.

How does that happen? You go through the gate, and you receive His righteousness. To come through the gate requires you to be humble, surrendering your will to His will. This is not a passive surrender, but a very active one. Each of us is called to come into agreement with God about His promises to us. Where will we find His promises? On the path. If you have a heart to go, He promises you the beautiful things of life. He will show you the way you personally are supposed to go. Do we all have the same way? No. It's His way for us, which is unique to each of us.

He promises to show you the way to go as well as His promises that are unique to your way. You'll be led to the abundance. Why? Because He is the good shepherd. He is going to show you secrets. He will command and reveal His Covenant. Your role is to come and be with Him within the life and promise of the Covenant. How do you fulfill your role to receive the Covenant? Follow Him. As stated in verse 15, your eyes are ever to be toward the Lord—keep looking to Him and staying with Him.

If we are to walk in the way of truth, what then is our prayer? How are we to remain in this place of following? What will be the benefit to me if I remain there?

> **Read Psalm 43:3–4:**
>
> [3] Send out your light and your truth;
>   let them lead me;
> let them bring me to your holy hill
>   and to your dwelling!
> [4] Then I will go to the altar of God,
>   to God my exceeding joy,
> and I will praise you with the lyre,
>   O God, my God.

____

____

____

____

____

Our prayer is for what? That You would give us light, give us truth. Illuminate us, lead us, and guide us. We need to be led. We are going to follow You. We are the sheep. We will follow Your voice. Lead us into the place where You are. We know it's holy and it's going to be spectacular. Please give us a heart to follow. If we have a heart to follow, He will lead and guide us—every step of the way.

Since we are in the world and will experience trouble along the way, what are we to do in this trouble? What does He then promise regarding this trouble? Why is this such an important aspect of remaining on the way?

Read Psalm 86:1–13:

Great Is Your Steadfast Love

A Prayer of David.

86 Incline your ear, O LORD, and answer me,
 for I am poor and needy.
2 Preserve my life, for I am godly;
 save your servant, who trusts in you—you are my God.
3 Be gracious to me, O Lord,
 for to you do I cry all the day.
4 Gladden the soul of your servant,
 for to you, O Lord, do I lift up my soul.
5 For you, O Lord, are good and forgiving,
 abounding in steadfast love to all who call upon you.
6 Give ear, O LORD, to my prayer;
 listen to my plea for grace.
7 In the day of my trouble I call upon you,
 for you answer me.
8 There is none like you among the gods, O Lord,
 nor are there any works like yours.
9 All the nations you have made shall come
 and worship before you, O Lord,
 and shall glorify your name.
10 For you are great and do wondrous things;
 you alone are God.
11 Teach me your way, O LORD,
 that I may walk in your truth;
 unite my heart to fear your name.

> ¹² I give thanks to you, O Lord my God, with my whole heart,
>   and I will glorify your name forever.
> ¹³ For great is your steadfast love toward me;
>   you have delivered my soul from the depths of Sheol.

This psalm describes what is normal for living in this world. If you have trouble in your life, what are you supposed to do? Go to Him, call out to Him, tell Him you need some help. He said that when you go to Him, He will answer you and show you the way to resolution. While He can certainly take care of any issue on His own, you are to be an active participant who walks with Him until your issue is resolved. As you are walking along that path and resolution is revealed to you, what will happen the next time trouble comes around? Instead of getting upset about the trouble, you will seek God and ask Him to show you the way because you know He has the answer.

Our prayer—this psalm—goes even deeper. We ask God to unite our heart with His so that we have a heart to follow Him. We ask to be made willing to follow Him. It is not only that though. Since He has all the answers, we ask what is important for us. We ask to be able to hear and clearly understand instruction so that we can take the right path and follow it step by step.

A friend was diagnosed with cancer, and he was looking at different therapies to get it resolved. His struggle was not about potentially dying from the cancer but rather the consequences of the therapy—the side effects that would dramatically impact his quality of life. In trying to find resolution, he asked God what path he should go on so that not only will the cancer be cured, but he won't have to deal with those negative consequences.

Together, we processed the way God instructed: ask, seek, knock, and then listen to what God has to say. This friend does his research and finds out there are 25 different therapies. Since God already knows which is the best path, the typical response would be to ask God to tell us which one. But, instead, God says *no* because He wants to take us down the path for us to discover the truth step by step.

We need to think differently. God says He is the way, and He has a path for you. There are steps along this path that He needs you to follow. In seeking God, you know that He will get you the answer, but you must follow the path.

This friend does additional research and finds that there are four or five treatments that have a higher probability of success than the other 20. He focuses on those, and after further digging, he learns that they're all about the same. There's not one that stands out as being better than the others. They all could have problems, but they all could be successful, as well. So he prays to God and asks the Father to show Him the way.

As he's seeking God's way, God starts to do supernatural things, and one therapy suddenly strikes him as interesting. The next day, another friend calls him up without prompting and asks if he has considered this certain therapy—the same one that had struck his heart. Through this person, God said, "Pay attention." Following that, one day he's driving home from the airport and sees a big billboard in Illinois. It advertises the exact therapy that he had noticed and was the one that his friend had mentioned. He was starting to see the path that God was revealing to him, but he had to remember that it was still just a path—he doesn't have his answer yet.

He didn't know if God was telling him to pursue this treatment or take it off the table. He needed to continue pursuing God in order to find God's answer. I advised him to focus on that one treatment to discover if this was the answer, another path to His true answer, or if there was a timing issue involved in this. He made several phone calls to this center, but received no response of any kind—nothing. Three weeks later, he calls me up and tells me that he has called them five times and has never received a phone call back, so he guesses this wasn't it. I stayed completely neutral and asked God what He had to say about this.

This is the beautiful role of fellowship and community. We are standing next to our fellow believer who is seeking God's will and we get to assist in the process. God told me to ask him if he was being disobedient to something that He asked him to do. When I asked him if he had been disobedient to something, the other end of the phone went silent. "Yes," he said quietly. When I asked him what it was, he said that God told him to tell the company he worked for that he had cancer, but he didn't want to until he discovered what the therapy was going to be and what was involved in it. At that point, he felt he could go and negotiate something with them.

But, God told him to go tell his company now. I asked him if he was willing to do this, and he said, "No." He was fearful of what they may do or may not do and how they were going to handle it, so he didn't want to do that. I then asked him if he was neutral, and he said, "No." I further advised him to spend time with God in his Gethsemane and work it through until he was willing to be neutral and had a willingness to hear and follow God's leading.

He takes a couple of weeks to work this through, and after processing with God, he gets to neutral where he trusts that God's truth is to be received and followed. I asked him what God reinforced with him, and he said he was to go tell his company. When I asked if he was willing to do that, he said, "I guess so, because I think I'm blocking the answer." Yes, that was exactly what was happening. He then asked me, "What should I ask the company for?" I told him to pray about it and I would do the same.

When we came back together, he said, "I received the funniest thing—God told me to say nothing." I told him I heard the same thing—that their answer will be God's answer. He wasn't to ask for anything—just tell them the truth of his situation, and then receive their response as God's answer.

After he tells his company, he called me and said that the leader of the company told him to take the entire year off. They would pay his full salary for the year and would not count it against any of his time. In addition, when he returns, he would re-enter his current position. He further said to enjoy the year with his spouse and to go get healed.

I asked him if he would have ever considered asking for all that, and he said, "No." God's way is always the best and none better. He also said that 45 minutes later, he received a phone call from the medical center. God was waiting for the obedience to take His way, His path, for His answer to be known. This friend received treatment and was healed. He suffered no side effects, and his quality of life was unaffected.

God's grace is the way, the truth, and the life. The way is a process of learning, discovery, and timing. He may want to teach you and impact an issue of your heart or thoughts, but it is always to lead you to His path of the Covenant—blessing you to make you a blessing. Don't worry about how things look right now because of the trouble that is part of the world. Instead, seek His help, His answers. He will get you what you need when you trust Him.

If we are walking God's way, what are all the benefits that we are assured to receive? What is our role to be able to receive these benefits? How then shall we expect life to be for us? Why?

Read Psalm 145:

Great Is the LORD

[a] A Song of Praise. Of David.

145 I will extol you, my God and King,
   and bless your name forever and ever.
2 Every day I will bless you
   and praise your name forever and ever.
3 Great is the LORD, and greatly to be praised,
   and his greatness is unsearchable.
4 One generation shall commend your works to another,
   and shall declare your mighty acts.
5 On the glorious splendor of your majesty,
   and on your wondrous works, I will meditate.
6 They shall speak of the might of your awesome deeds,
   and I will declare your greatness.
7 They shall pour forth the fame of your abundant goodness
   and shall sing aloud of your righteousness.
8 The LORD is gracious and merciful,
   slow to anger and abounding in steadfast love.
9 The LORD is good to all,
   and his mercy is over all that he has made.
10 All your works shall give thanks to you, O LORD,
   and all your saints shall bless you!
11 They shall speak of the glory of your kingdom
   and tell of your power,
12 to make known to the children of man your[b] mighty deeds,
   and the glorious splendor of your kingdom.

---

¹³ Your kingdom is an everlasting kingdom,
and your dominion endures throughout all generations.
[The LORD is faithful in all his words
and kind in all his works.][c]
¹⁴ The LORD upholds all who are falling
and raises up all who are bowed down.
¹⁵ The eyes of all look to you,
and you give them their food in due season.
¹⁶ You open your hand;
you satisfy the desire of every living thing.
¹⁷ The LORD is righteous in all his ways
and kind in all his works.
¹⁸ The LORD is near to all who call on him,
to all who call on him in truth.
¹⁹ He fulfills the desire of those who fear him;
he also hears their cry and saves them.
²⁰ The LORD preserves all who love him,
but all the wicked he will destroy.
²¹ My mouth will speak the praise of the LORD,
and let all flesh bless his holy name forever and ever.

This psalm speaks to God's magnificence. He is wonderful, supernatural, favor. Who is this magnificence toward? Everybody, all His children. That's His heart. It is Covenant loyalty. The word *mercy* used in this psalm means Covenant loyalty. God is loyal to the Covenant, and He will deliver the Covenant to you. It's available for everybody.

Why is it available to everyone? Because He is the way, and if you follow Him, He is going to deliver that—always. It's available to everybody who has a heart to go. God says, "This is My heart, because 'I am' the life, 'I am' the resurrection."

As we experience this beautiful resurrection life that God offers each of us, we are to praise Him—giving Him honor and glory. We did not receive it because we were lucky or we figured this out on our own, rather, this was God—it was supernatural—it was something only God could do. Praising Him also draws us into His bigger story of giving it away—bearing witness to God's resurrection life. When others see the truth of this, they will ask if it is possible for them, too. When we praise God in an effervescent way that others can see, then other people are going to catch it.

As we learn to fully understand this, we can confidently guarantee that others can also experience this life. Why? Because of the nature of God. He's the great "I am." In the middle of trouble, we all have the same opportunity to go be with God. We can help others learn to be with Him, as well. We don't have the answers that others seek, but we can show them that if they're with Him, He has the answers and will resolve their trouble.

LESSON 3:
"I AM" THE TRUE VINE

The Vine:

What does "Jesus is the vine" mean? What does that provide to us? What is the relationship between the vine and the vinedresser? What does that mean for us? What is our role, and what choice do we make? What are the benefits of making this choice? Why?

Read John 15:1–8:

I Am the True Vine

15 "I am the true vine, and my Father is the vinedresser. [2] Every branch in me that does not bear fruit he takes away, and every branch that does bear fruit he prunes, that it may bear more fruit. [3] Already you are clean because of the word that I have spoken to you. [4] Abide in me, and I in you. As the branch cannot bear fruit by itself, unless it abides in the vine, neither can you, unless you abide in me. [5] I am the vine; you are the branches. Whoever abides in me and I in him, he it is that bears much fruit, for apart from me you can do nothing. [6] If anyone does not abide in me he is thrown away like a branch and withers; and the branches are gathered, thrown into the fire, and burned. [7] If you abide in me, and my words abide in you, ask whatever you wish, and it will be done for you. [8] By this my Father is glorified, that you bear much fruit and so prove to be my disciples.

____

____

____

____

____

From our course in abiding, "Abiding in the Vine," we know this truth: Jesus says, "I am the true vine." What does the vine do? It gives life. Jesus is the giver of His wonderful life and all the elements we have learned thus far in this course. His Father is the what? The vinedresser is who is going to orchestrate everything for each of us to live connected to Him—to lead and guide us to the way of experiencing His life. Your role is simply to abide in the vine and stay connected.

When you abide in the vine, how often are you connected? Every moment of every day—24 hours a day, seven days a week. It's a relationship. We talk a lot about abiding in the Word, and that's critical, but it's not just a Bible study. It's abiding in the relationship, the life of Christ. When? One hundred percent of the time—all the time. When you are in this type of relationship, He can check you before you make a poor decision; He can correct you; He can speak to you; He can interrupt you; He can encourage you. He can do all these things because you're connected. When you are connected, you are living in freedom, and you are enjoying the life that He is giving you—including transforming your character.

Jesus says that apart from Him, you can do what? Nothing. It is a choice. If you choose not to abide, there is no life, you die, and are then discarded. It is critical for you to experience all that He is. We are to learn to abide in the Vine. He goes on to say that if you abide in Him and His words—the bread—abide in you, you can do what? Pray what He has spoken and see it happen as promised—to bear much fruit. By this, His Father is glorified. How? His supernatural work changes circumstances—nothing is too difficult for Him. He is the fruit of life.

As we abide in the vine, we are on God's path. We have learned that there will be trouble, loss, difficult circumstances—even those that we caused ourselves because we were not walking on His path. First, what is required for us to return to the path? Why is this so important when we are in the middle of difficulty? If we return, what does God promise? What can we then expect about the resolution to our difficulty? Why?

Read Joel 2:22–32:

22 Fear not, you beasts of the field,
   for the pastures of the wilderness are green;
the tree bears its fruit;
   the fig tree and vine give their full yield.
23 "Be glad, O children of Zion,
   and rejoice in the LORD your God,
for he has given the early rain for your vindication;
   he has poured down for you abundant rain,
   the early and the latter rain, as before.
24 "The threshing floors shall be full of grain;
   the vats shall overflow with wine and oil.
25 I will restore[a] to you the years

that the swarming locust has eaten,
the hopper, the destroyer, and the cutter,
    my great army, which I sent among you.
26 "You shall eat in plenty and be satisfied,
    and praise the name of the LORD your God,
    who has dealt wondrously with you.
And my people shall never again be put to shame.
27 You shall know that I am in the midst of Israel,
    and that I am the LORD your God and there is none else.
And my people shall never again be put to shame.

The LORD Will Pour Out His Spirit
28 [b] "And it shall come to pass afterward,
    that I will pour out my Spirit on all flesh;
your sons and your daughters shall prophesy,
    your old men shall dream dreams,
    and your young men shall see visions.
29 Even on the male and female servants
    in those days I will pour out my Spirit.

30 "And I will show wonders in the heavens and on the earth, blood and fire and columns of smoke. 31 The sun shall be turned to darkness, and the moon to blood, before the great and awesome day of the LORD comes. 32 And it shall come to pass that everyone who calls on the name of the LORD shall be saved. For in Mount Zion and in Jerusalem there shall be those who escape, as the Lord has said, and among the survivors shall be those whom the LORD calls.

We have learned that abiding in Christ, the vine, will produce results, fruit. He describes it as super abundance, and it is going to happen for you. He knows that one of our issues in life is doubt: This sounds really good, but I've lost stuff and ruined stuff, and life isn't quite what I thought it was going to be. God understands that and still offers His way—the life of the resurrection that can restore to you what has been lost or ruined. He will restore it when you decide to come and abide with Him. That's the beauty of the gospel. There is nothing that God can't restore, no matter how bad it seems to us. Yes, you made a mess of it, and you've got a big problem that you can't get over. God knows about all of it, and still pursues a relationship with you. None of this stops Him from restoring to you the beauty and the wonder of the full restoration. Whatever you've lost, I'll restore it and make it even better. This is the Covenant.

As in Joel, God promises to restore to us what is lost. What are the four things He promises, and what do they mean in our practical lives? What then are our three responsibilities to receive these promises? What do each look like in our practical lives? If we fulfill this and receive these promises, what will we experience as part of God's bigger story? Why is this so important?

Read Zechariah 8:11–23:

[11] But now I will not deal with the remnant of this people as in the former days, declares the LORD of hosts. [12] For there shall be a sowing of peace. The vine shall give its fruit, and the ground shall give its produce, and the heavens shall give their dew. And I will cause the remnant of this people to possess all these things. [13] And as you have been a byword of cursing among the nations, O house of Judah and house of Israel, so will I save you, and you shall be a blessing. Fear not, but let your hands be strong."

[14] For thus says the LORD of hosts: "As I purposed to bring disaster to you when your fathers provoked me to wrath, and I did not relent, says the LORD of hosts, [15] so again have I purposed in these days to bring good to Jerusalem and to the house of Judah; fear not. [16] These are the things that you shall do: Speak the truth to one another; render in your gates judgments that are true and make for peace; [17] do not devise evil in your hearts against one another, and love no false oath, for all these things I hate, declares the LORD."

> [18] And the word of the LORD of hosts came to me, saying, [19] "Thus says the LORD of hosts: The fast of the fourth month and the fast of the fifth and the fast of the seventh and the fast of the tenth shall be to the house of Judah seasons of joy and gladness and cheerful feasts. Therefore love truth and peace.
>
> [20] "Thus says the LORD of hosts: Peoples shall yet come, even the inhabitants of many cities. [21] The inhabitants of one city shall go to another, saying, 'Let us go at once to entreat the favor of the LORD and to seek the LORD of hosts; I myself am going.' [22] Many peoples and strong nations shall come to seek the LORD of hosts in Jerusalem and to entreat the favor of the LORD. [23] Thus says the LORD of hosts: In those days ten men from the nations of every tongue shall take hold of the robe of a Jew, saying, 'Let us go with you, for we have heard that God is with you.'"

____

____

____

____

____

God defines the full aspect of restoration.

1. The seed will be prosperous. His Word, the bread, will fulfill what He has to say. You'll receive all that He speaks.

2. The vine will produce its fruit—the fruit of holiness, the fruit of changed circumstances. You will experience all that God wants to give you of the super-abundant life.

3. Your ground and your livestock are going to be prosperous. The things of life that you need for living will be given to you super abundantly—and not just materially, but all aspects of your life will have abundance.

4. He will give you the dew, the refreshment, which is the Holy Spirit. He is going to give you the life of the Holy Spirit that you will fully experience.

He reiterates that He is committed to delivering this to you, and you can be confident of it because of His Covenant loyalty. He is going to give you the Covenant and all of this will be fulfilled if you have a heart to be with Him. He then says that your role is to do what?

1. Speak the truth. Help each other with truth. Be led into truth.

2. Don't speak evil by speaking against each other and complaining, but rather lift each other up and encourage each other that the Covenant is sure, available, and for everyone.

3. Don't make a false vow. What is a false vow? Saying you'll do something, but you don't. Saying you are going to follow Him, but you don't. Vowing to abide in Him, but you don't. He says: Don't make a false vow—rather commit to follow Him and stay with Him. He will give you the power to stay with Him.

Following this, there are a number of fasts and feasts to join. These celebrations always started with a fast and a sacrifice. In order to enter into the bounty, you have to do what? You have to sacrifice your will for His, then you can enjoy the feasting and celebration. When you're celebrating, as is described in Psalm 145, what are you doing? Praising Him openly because of His wondrous works that are directed toward you. As you do this, what part of God's bigger story do we get to experience? Other people wanting to join us in living life in the resurrection. This happens when they see the work of God in our lives. It isn't what you personally have done, they are seeing that God is demonstrating His life in your life. They can see that God is with you, and they want to be where God is. If they ask to join you, they are not asking to follow you or your system or the things that are happening to you, but rather to learn so they, too, can experience the life of God. There is the beautiful purpose of it all.

In Israel, whenever they had a feast, did they do it by themselves? No. It was always in fellowship where they share what God is doing. It's not theoretical, nor mechanical. It's real and authentic. It's joyful and fantastic, and you get to express it when you're walking with Him and experiencing the life that God gives.

People who need discipling usually come across your path because they're in trouble or are having problems or difficulties. Whatever the issue, there is doubt keeping them from truly seeking God for the answers to their issues. But, if you know the "I am," you also know that He is the bread of life, the light of the world, the gate, and the good shepherd. He is the resurrection. He is the way, the truth, and the life. He is the vine, and He can't alter who He is. Knowing this, you can help others fulfill the requirement that is their role. What is their role? Just to be with Him. If they have a heart to go, you can help them learn to abide in Him. Help them learn that if they join the Kingdom and surrender their will, God will fulfill His promise. He will speak. He will do miracles. They will see that this is real and will work hard to continue along His path. They will also see their problems being resolved.

An executive I was discipling learned this, and as his problems were resolved and God's supernatural work led him to Covenant life, he gave it away to others. He shared an example with me. A friend of his was a documentary filmmaker who went to Canada and got paid $300,000 to do a documentary. When he gets to Canada, he has this conversation with God:

God: What are you doing?

Filmmaker: I'm making $300,000 to do a documentary.

God: Did you check in with Me? I don't want you to make this documentary. You are promoting things that aren't good. I don't want you doing it.

Filmmaker: So, You want me to forego $300,000 and not do this?

God: Exactly.

So, he calls up his friend, the executive I had been discipling, and said, "I heard God say this, but I'm not sure about it. It doesn't make sense. I thought this documentary was a good thing—certainly the pay was good. Could you help confirm it?" The executive goes to prayer and confirmed what the filmmaker heard. God also spoke to him and told him that his friend was not supposed to do this. He confirmed that it was God's will for him to give up that $300,000.

So, he went to the Canadian government and told them that he was not going to make the documentary after all. He offered to help find somebody who could but that he personally could not do it. After this, he asked God what He wanted him to do. God said, "I want you to make a documentary about the impact of abortion on the husband." He then asked how he would do that, and God told him that He would show him.

He went on to make this amazing documentary, and through his research, he realized that the impact on the woman is obviously significant, but the impact on the husband is just as significant, if not more. This filmmaker was led by God to make a documentary for His purpose. If he was willing, God was going to bless him financially, restoring all that he had lost.

All of this was set into motion when the executive and his wife attended a retreat and learned to abide and receive the abundant life of God. Others, including this filmmaker, saw this change, and asked if they, too, could experience this. They could see that God was with them, which ultimately results in the number of followers multiplying.

God is the "I am." He can't be anything else. If you seek Him and live His way, on His path, you will experience this, too. It will be enjoyable and super abundant for you and even more wonderful when your passion for Christ leads others into the Kingdom.

As we finish this course, *The Life of Jesus—I Am,* let's understand how simple this is and how beautiful it is. When John wrote, *The Gospel of John,* he set out to understand that Jesus is the "I am." We are to experience the fullness of the life of the "I am." We have to walk with Him and receive the "I am"—"I am" the bread of life; "I am" the light of the world; "I am" the gate; "I am" the good shepherd. "I am" the resurrection; "I am" the way, the truth, and the life. "I am" the vine. We are simply to be with Him, and He, being the "I am" who does not change, makes this life available to all of us who have a heart to go. May we all experience this.